Instructions for Lies and Flowers
POEMS FOR SUNDAY'S CHILD
MILLER ADAMS

www.crowecreations.ca

Instructions for Lies and Flowers: Poems for Sunday's Child
© 2019, Miller Adams

First Crowe Creations Publication November 2019

Cover photo © iStock photo ID: 113536898; Credit: TShum
Cover Design © 2019 Crowe Creations
Interior design by Crowe Creations
Text set in Backtalk Serif BTN; headings in Firenze SF

Crowe Creations
ISBN: 978-1-927058-62-6

To my Darlings

Jane, Michael, Danny and Meredith

. . . alone at night, we waken

to the scent of flowers

lying in the shards of broken dreams.

— Louise McDiarmid, "Riding the 85 Bus",

HEARD INSTINCT, Pachyderm Poets, 2005, ADAR Press

Table of Contents

Night Letter, unsent

If I could say anything to you — and since
you'll never see this, I will —
I'd say parenthood is an addiction.
I begged; you didn't ask to be born.
Forgive me for not explaining:
I didn't know the language.
When Rilke said, every Angel is terrifying,
I think he meant the thunderous beating of wings,
in the moment before we see them,
when the light hurts our eyes.
They've touched God, don't understand the *pain*
of light. And they no more wish to be born as man
than we yearn to come back to earth
as snails that snuff across the aquarium glass.

Who said our children are lent to us?
We can let go so easily. You grew up,
out of reach; I grew down, inward,
rooted in questions that had no answers.
We pare our stories to the bone,
make of our grief a metaphor,
draw Angels in to fill up the awkward spaces.
feeling safest with those who no longer remember
anything, and those still learning the words.
So you and I don't talk of these things; honesty blinds
but so does hope. And the shortest path
may be only a holding pattern.

If those Angels wept for Lilith, why not for you?
I want to know if they slip through windows
of dreams, or on nights when you can't sleep,
weave the darkness into illusion — or safer realities.
I'm still here for you, flawed and unschooled
as I always was, drinking my coffee,
stroking the cat, picking dead leaves,
trying to stare down the night from my kitchen window
and missing you.
Sleep well, my love. I send you all my Angels.

Sunday's Child I

For the years I spent wanting to know you.
For the months I spent knitting, mint green —
     not knowing.
For the day we met, your white eyelashes.
For the flurry of perfect names.
For the blanket you carried everywhere.
For the books I bought you and read myself
     and read to you, and read again
     and you saved them for your own child.
     For colouring inside the lines.
For the mornings you shaved ice off the inside windshield
     while I put my foot to the floor,
     the town clock striking.
For ballet and figure skating and the biggest cookie in the world.
For all the times you came first and the time they said
     you had to learn to come second
     and you told them you already knew that.
For the time you said, *If I die, will you come with me?*

Last Born

Who will remember that Sunday:
your lashes were white,
white your hair, duck's down,

only the crown darker.
But the nurse said that was the colour
your full head of hair would be.

Within days your lashes were dark
and the down: erased by soft hands
that stroked you?

The brown hair grew long
and thick, a shawl protective
and private.

I wanted to give you years
of long mornings,
a house with safe rooms,

floors swept clean of old sorrows,
books that don't let you sleep
without them.

But I wonder if even then you
plotted escape, drawing a curtain
between us, harbouring secret choices:

darker paths, inscrutable privacies.

Sometimes, you whisper
*I don't know where I leave off
and the world begins*

The Words Left Over Orphaned at the Table

Afraid of butterflies, you stay indoors.
a bowl of soup, a cappuccino coffee.
half-line, caesura, wander-thoughts consumed.
the world she fears is knocking at the door.
hair, smelling of toast crumbs, amber mornings
grandma's apron baskets eggs and plums.
Saturday brings strawberries on ice,
summer scents, days of liquorice pipes.
cotton candy fields down by the tracks.
all that is left are churches without pews.

you fly tomorrow after sleepless nights.

Without Night there can be no Day, without Day no Night

Years ago, you could wake up from a dream
and the dream would stay
on the pillow, sunlight
would bleach it into oblivion
though sometimes a thread or two would cling
like cat's hair to a sweater.

One day your dreams swarmed like a pack of wild dogs,
tore through the hours, devoured innocent chunks
of raw beginnings — essays   interviews   poems
cantatas   faery tales — long
journeys to safe places.

The world purged itself into your brain,
every little self swept with earth's effluvia
down a black hole.

You never saw it coming and such a long way back

Epiphany

You're reading *The Dead* and *Death in Jerusalem*,
all those cheery vicissitudes in Irish Lit.
Last winter your laptop was stolen,
now it's your USB, your bag of stories.
Travelling under a black cloud:
things die, disappear. Nothing returns.

In the East, the cherry blossoms
hold their branches for seventeen syllables
before they drop. Spontaneous perfection
right down to the Basho moment.

A supper of pizza, the cold dark walk.
A cat follows you home, curls up on your legs
through the night, refuses to leave
in the morning. Humbles, insinuates,
purrs miming mercy, mercy,
feed me.

Sunday's Child II

For the monster in the mirror.
For the times you went missing.
For the psychologist who lived on Coca Cola and nicotine
        and drove his car into a tree.
For the snipers on nearby rooftops.
For the pills.
For the phone calls and the phone calls and the phone calls.
For the silence

Cinquain

too soon
you tell me you're
in your life's November
handfuls of pills to help you through
the night

I worry about you

when it's snowing you can't find your boots your coat doesn't fit
a button is lost the bus is late dark out and such a long way. I
worry about you at class at home at the coffee shop a rally a
reading a rave a restlessness too little too much to remember. I
worry about you always losing money books friends I worry
about you all 350 pages so many unread and no translation. I
worry about the illness yours everyone's no yours when others
descend ignoring my limits the day I may say take your illness
somewhere else I will be lonely bereft I will be old unable this
darkness too light to sleep in something wild slipping through
open windows and under doors. I worry about you shaking snow
from your shoulders feet like ice the phone rings the message
comes on so tired so pale so *not you*

I worry about you worrying. I worry about *why* and tight-jawed
lies tangled truths you caught in the middle long skirt hand-me-
down smile shawl to massage and gloves without fingers and
histories written rewritten sepia photos old and brittle the cat on
the broken fence the children one in front of the other you in my
arms how many steps across the yard behind the house into the
woods miles in a night where the road disappears when the
stars won't give up the dark and it's so damn cold every letter of
the alphabet turns blue. I worry about how to tell you that
writing a poem should never be the sum of all its partings a lost
poem can never be found in
                    tact life is cheap death is so expensive

Too Wet to Walk in the Woods
for A.

Friends beyond lying, we talked of our children
or mostly yours, early risers in safe countries
while we washed luncheon dishes in a big plastic bowl.
I washed; you dried. It was like the old days
and the years slipped away from our hands.
I felt lighter and just for a moment forgot
all that I packed and brought to your cottage.

Then the rain came, and thunder and lightning.
The garden and the shed and the gravel path
were scoured clean and the whole world was clean.
All in a moment my heart opened like
the wing-flutter of a quick umbrella
and I was happy to stay indoors, to watch
summer through a pane of glass
with clean hands and yesterday far behind.

We walked lightly on the Earth, didn't leave a Mark

Here's to the secondary life,
the elusive one that yesterday crossed the street
and before the light could change entered a warm dark alley
that welcomed it like the hug of a long-lost brother.

The clouds are fat and oblivious
duvets for cold gods;
you fear they will wipe you out
like the classmate who never remembered your name.

The sister rain insists it's time:
let me bathe you with angel hands;
the darkness will towel you dry
and bundle you into the soil.

Raise your hand my love if you think that the system is working

Unknown, this Girl

The unidentified body of a girl
is found in a ditch. For two
months her face rates prime-time,
air-brushed to unscarred serenity,
eyes looking into ours.
Then policemen bear her body
coffined, unsung, to her grave.
The only family she has.
And hundreds of grieving parents
all over the country let
out their breaths, smooth rag
doll flounces on pillows, leave
porch lights burning.

Unknown, this girl, forever.
But you: sudden dreams swell
the full moon of your innocence
and you vanish without a trace.
Again and again.
The primal drumbeats of your rage
spell motive and opportunity;
no weapon will ever be found,
the echoes already dying
before the hunt begins.

You wear a cross, know nothing
of fragmented bone rejoined
in stuttering questions.
You, shaped by a name, yet nameless
in fury, the mirrored face you cannot
live with leaving no clue. Does it

help to say I love you? To say,
your room is just as you left it?
Dust prints of butterflies pattern
the window that frames these fearful
journeys; your photograph stares
me down; a key turns in the lock, who
is it returns to the scene of the crime
alone and unrelenting?

Your Hair at the End of my Life

Thirty years from now I am on my death bed
and you come to see me and take
my hand and sit watching me
and we are strangers.
I say to you, *So this is the end of the story.*
Knowing if it is the end for me it is the end
all the end I know or need to know
all the end I ever will know
and the rest doesn't matter.
And you squeeze my hand and say nothing
and I say, *Your hair is grey.*
and shake my head sadly, mystified.
I do not say, You are not my daughter.

Or it is next year
and I am on my death bed
and you come to see me and take
my hand and sit watching me.
And I notice that you have tied your hair back
with a bright ribbon
and I see that is the measure of your love for me.
And we are still strangers.

The Sad Architecture of Enabling

I.

Home for the day. A trial run.
Let me rub your feet. Bring coffee.
> *No cell phones, videos, scissors, matches,*
> *vitamins. Hospital gowns only.*

I want to bring you an armful of tulips,
massage away your hurt,
close the drapes so the darkness is gentle,
open the balcony door just a crack
so the air is fresh not serrated, not
> *Relapsed, locked up. No visitors. No privileges.*
> *Staff regulations.*

a knife on your pale wounded skin

> *Please hold, your call is important to us.*

II.

Be nice to your doctor,
the social worker,
the woman at the welfare office.
Be polite. Grateful.
If all else fails, cry.

> *The office is closed on Fridays.*

Sunday's Child III

For the bear who spoke for both of us when we didn't know
    what to say.

For the day you threw out your childhood.

For the play you wrote and wouldn't let me read.

For the time you cut all your hair off.

For the handcuffs.

For the needles.

For the pills.

For your friend who jumped off the roof of the hospital parking
    garage.

For the day all your things were stolen and replaced with exact
    replicas.

For the journeys in search of healers.

For the ones we haven't found yet.

For the pills.

I Try My Hand at the Art of Forgetting

We can hardly remember the days before
life was running away with us;
when you wrote of forgetting, ineptly,
as currency for survival.
Practised forgetting to make it
dissolve the seasons
like the blue, consumptive angel
Monet might have painted
had he painted angels.
Memory running like water down glass.
The artist never lies but doesn't always
remember.

Rivers dried up and landslides banged the earth
like a fool's head on a stone wall.
Years fled, skin slackened and words grew
frantic to marshal resistance, begging
to be anthologized. Every word for itself.
Poems broke ranks, slipped into cracks and down drains,
a word here a word there
forget me
not

There are times when we want to remember:
angels in graveyards, a humble scatter of footprints;
days when our future was nothing
more than a desperate caution.
How quickly they rose and fell,
how soon we looked for our past
in a little heap of stones.

Now we simply forget;
our lives have got beyond us
untethered netherness —
petal and fledgling, bone from the dog star.

Your Phone Call

As if you wakened from a bad dream —
a friend replaced with an impostor
and the two of them fighting until
Someone Who Ruled The Earth
commanded you to stop.
A dream where your mother
the Antichrist runs a satanic ring
and only a monosyllabic chant
can ward her off.

You want me to talk to your doctor.
I say, the staff won't listen to me,
you've told them all I'm evil.
Oh, Mom, you say, *they don't believe
crazy people.
They hear that all the time.*

Instructions for Lies and Flowers

When I die, let me lie in a plain wood box.
Let children bring flowers from the fields
blue and purple and white.
A sprig of green.
Let there be dancing and good wine
and someone singing off-key.

Tell the children I'm up *there*
if it makes them happy.
They need to sleep safe at night.
They need to sleep well.
And once in a while, on a morning
when vines part and the sun rushes in
they might raise their eyes
to the heavens and smile. Wave, perhaps.

Don't take them to the grave site
with its small, unobtrusive slab
unless they beg you to let them
rub secrets from chiseled stone
and run their fingers through earth.
And limit your lies lest a day comes
when they turn on you.

I had a little life:
a very small soul fitted into that space
reserved for the chronically lost and bewildered.
My love, if I die — if I die! — will you come with me?

Let no one who knew me think I'm at peace
lying mute and unanswered
for I won't be there;
I won't be back.

Sunday's Child IV

For the birthday portrait you painted of me, the eyes.
For the poems you write.
For the children you never had, the perfect names.

Acknowledgements

To a multitude of friends and fellow writers with whom I've read, workshopped and celebrated the written word over decades. Particularly notable are members of Ottawa's Field Stone Poets, Pachyderm Poets, and Monday Afternoon Poetry and Prose Writers, past and present all — once a member, the door is always open.

And special thanks to Sherrill Wark for her unfailing advice, encouragement and expertise, and for holding this technically bewildered and unschooled writer's hand throughout this undertaking.

About the Author

Miller Adams's poetry collection, *Folding Laundry on Judgment Day*, is forthcoming from Aeolus House in 2020. Two children's friendly witch stories, illustrated by Brandon Chung, will also appear. Previously writing as Sylvia Adams, she published a novel, *This Weather of Hangmen*, poetry collections *Sleeping on the Moon* (runner-up for the Archibald Lampman prize), *Mondrian's Elephant* (Cranberry Tree Press 1998 winner), and a children's book, *Dinner at the Dog Pound*. A book reviewer, she was also poetry editor for the *Ottawa Citizen*. As a founding member of Ottawa's Field Stone Poets, her poems appear in their chapbooks and their anthology *Whistle for Jellyfish*. Numerous awards include the Diana Brebner Prize, two Aesthetica International Poetry Awards (2012 and 2013), and Canadian Authors Association prizes. Her work appears in over thirty literary magazines including *Queen's Quarterly, Arc Poetry Magazine, The New Quarterly*, and League of Canadian Poets *Vintage* anthologies. She has led writing groups in Canada and Chile and been published in Canada, England, the United States and South America. She is an introvert, synesthete, vegetarian, bibliophile, ailurophile, dedicated Luddite and one of the last Victorians.

www.ingramcontent.com/pod-product-compliance
Lightning Source LLC
Chambersburg PA
CBHW060648030426
42337CB00018B/3504